50 Premium Lunch Recipes for Home

By: Kelly Johnson

Table of Contents

- Grilled Salmon Nicoise Salad
- Lobster Roll with Garlic Butter
- Truffle Risotto with Wild Mushrooms
- Quinoa Stuffed Bell Peppers
- Shrimp Scampi Linguine
- Pan-Seared Tuna Steak with Mango Salsa
- Chicken Caesar Salad with Avocado Dressing
- Beef Wellington with Red Wine Reduction
- Caprese Panini with Balsamic Glaze
- Seafood Paella
- Thai Beef Salad with Peanut Dressing
- Lobster Bisque Soup
- Spinach and Feta Stuffed Chicken Breast
- Crab Cakes with Remoulade Sauce
- Mediterranean Veggie Wrap with Hummus
- Steak Fajita Bowl with Guacamole
- Vegetable Stir-Fry with Cashew Nuts
- Greek Orzo Salad with Lemon Vinaigrette
- Pesto Chicken Sandwich with Sun-Dried Tomatoes
- Teriyaki Salmon Bowl with Sesame Seeds
- Roasted Butternut Squash Soup with Sage Croutons
- Pan-Seared Scallops with Lemon Butter Sauce
- Ratatouille with Garlic Crostini
- BBQ Pulled Pork Sandwich with Coleslaw
- Sushi Burrito with Spicy Mayo
- Mushroom Risotto with Parmesan Crisps
- Tofu Buddha Bowl with Tahini Dressing
- Chicken Piccata with Capers
- Lobster Mac and Cheese
- Thai Green Curry with Tofu and Vegetables
- Prosciutto-Wrapped Asparagus with Balsamic Glaze
- Mediterranean Grilled Veggie Sandwich
- Beef Bulgogi Bibimbap Bowl
- Avocado and Tomato Gazpacho
- Pesto Pasta Salad with Cherry Tomatoes

- Crab Stuffed Avocado
- Smoked Salmon Bagel with Cream Cheese
- Vegetable Frittata with Goat Cheese
- Spicy Tuna Poke Bowl
- Roast Beef and Arugula Sandwich with Horseradish Aioli
- Sweet Potato and Black Bean Quesadilla
- Mediterranean Couscous Salad with Olives and Feta
- Thai Coconut Curry Soup with Shrimp
- Teriyaki Chicken Lettuce Wraps
- Quinoa Salad with Roasted Vegetables and Feta
- Caprese Salad with Balsamic Glaze
- Beef Tenderloin Salad with Blue Cheese Dressing
- Falafel Wrap with Tahini Sauce
- Chicken Satay Skewers with Peanut Sauce
- Veggie Sushi Bowl with Ginger Soy Dressing

Grilled Salmon Nicoise Salad

Ingredients:

- 1 lb fresh salmon fillets
- 2 tablespoons olive oil
- Salt and pepper to taste
- 4 cups mixed salad greens
- 1 cup cherry tomatoes, halved
- 1 cup cooked green beans, trimmed
- 4 hard-boiled eggs, halved
- 1/2 cup Niçoise olives
- 1/4 cup capers
- 4 small potatoes, boiled and quartered
- 2 tablespoons chopped fresh parsley (optional)
- Lemon wedges for serving

For the dressing:

- 1/4 cup extra virgin olive oil
- 2 tablespoons red wine vinegar
- 1 teaspoon Dijon mustard
- 1 garlic clove, minced
- Salt and pepper to taste

Instructions:

Preheat the grill to medium-high heat. Brush the salmon fillets with olive oil and season with salt and pepper.

Grill the salmon for 4-5 minutes per side, or until cooked through and nicely charred. Remove from the grill and set aside to cool slightly.

In a small bowl, whisk together the ingredients for the dressing: olive oil, red wine vinegar, Dijon mustard, minced garlic, salt, and pepper. Set aside.

In a large salad bowl, arrange the mixed salad greens as the base.

Arrange the cherry tomatoes, cooked green beans, hard-boiled eggs, Niçoise olives, capers, and boiled potatoes on top of the salad greens.

Flake the grilled salmon into large pieces and place them on the salad.

Drizzle the dressing over the salad and gently toss to combine.

Sprinkle chopped fresh parsley over the salad if desired.

Serve the Grilled Salmon Niçoise Salad with lemon wedges on the side. Enjoy!

Lobster Roll with Garlic Butter

Ingredients:

- 1 lb cooked lobster meat, chopped into bite-sized pieces
- 4 to 6 brioche hot dog rolls or split-top rolls
- 4 tablespoons unsalted butter
- 2 cloves garlic, minced
- 2 tablespoons chopped fresh parsley
- Salt and pepper to taste
- Juice of 1 lemon
- Optional: Chopped chives or green onions for garnish

Instructions:

In a large skillet over medium heat, melt the butter. Add the minced garlic and cook for 1-2 minutes until fragrant.

Add the chopped lobster meat to the skillet and toss to coat with the garlic butter. Cook for 2-3 minutes, just until the lobster meat is heated through. Be careful not to overcook.

Stir in the chopped parsley and season with salt and pepper to taste. Squeeze the lemon juice over the lobster mixture and stir to combine.

While the lobster is cooking, lightly toast the brioche rolls under the broiler or on a grill until golden brown.

Once the rolls are toasted, divide the warm lobster mixture evenly among them, spooning it into the rolls.

Garnish with chopped chives or green onions if desired.

Serve the Lobster Rolls with Garlic Butter immediately, with extra lemon wedges on the side if desired. Enjoy the luxurious flavors!

Truffle Risotto with Wild Mushrooms

Ingredients:

- 1 cup Arborio rice
- 4 cups vegetable or chicken broth
- 1 cup assorted wild mushrooms (such as shiitake, oyster, and cremini), sliced
- 2 shallots, finely chopped
- 2 cloves garlic, minced
- 1/4 cup dry white wine
- 2 tablespoons truffle oil
- 2 tablespoons olive oil
- 1/2 cup grated Parmesan cheese (optional)
- Salt and pepper to taste
- Chopped fresh parsley for garnish

Instructions:

In a medium saucepan, heat the vegetable or chicken broth over medium heat. Once heated, reduce the heat to low to keep it warm.

In a large skillet or sauté pan, heat the olive oil over medium heat. Add the chopped shallots and minced garlic, and cook until softened, about 2-3 minutes. Add the sliced wild mushrooms to the skillet and cook until they are golden brown and tender, about 5-6 minutes. Season with salt and pepper to taste.

Push the mushrooms to one side of the skillet and add the Arborio rice to the other side. Toast the rice for 1-2 minutes until it becomes lightly golden, stirring occasionally.

Pour the white wine into the skillet and stir, scraping any browned bits from the bottom of the pan. Allow the wine to cook until it has mostly evaporated.

Begin adding the warm broth to the skillet, one ladleful at a time, stirring constantly and allowing the rice to absorb the broth before adding more. Continue this process until the rice is creamy and cooked al dente, about 18-20 minutes.

Stir in the truffle oil and grated Parmesan cheese (if using), and adjust the seasoning with salt and pepper to taste.

Remove the skillet from the heat and let the risotto rest for a few minutes to allow the flavors to meld together.

Serve the Truffle Risotto with Wild Mushrooms hot, garnished with chopped fresh parsley. Enjoy the luxurious flavors and creamy texture of this indulgent dish!

Quinoa Stuffed Bell Peppers

Ingredients:

- 4 large bell peppers (any color), halved and seeds removed
- 1 cup quinoa, rinsed
- 2 cups vegetable broth or water
- 1 tablespoon olive oil
- 1 onion, diced
- 2 cloves garlic, minced
- 1 cup diced tomatoes (fresh or canned)
- 1 cup cooked black beans (canned or cooked from dry)
- 1 cup corn kernels (fresh, canned, or frozen)
- 1 teaspoon ground cumin
- 1 teaspoon paprika
- Salt and pepper to taste
- 1/2 cup shredded vegan cheese (optional)
- Fresh cilantro or parsley for garnish

Instructions:

Preheat the oven to 375°F (190°C). Place the halved bell peppers cut side up in a baking dish, and set aside.

In a medium saucepan, bring the vegetable broth or water to a boil. Add the rinsed quinoa, reduce the heat to low, cover, and simmer for about 15 minutes, or until the quinoa is cooked and the liquid is absorbed. Remove from heat and fluff with a fork.

In a large skillet, heat the olive oil over medium heat. Add the diced onion and cook until softened, about 5 minutes. Add the minced garlic and cook for an additional minute.

Stir in the diced tomatoes, black beans, corn kernels, ground cumin, paprika, salt, and pepper. Cook for 5-7 minutes, or until the mixture is heated through and the flavors are well combined.

Add the cooked quinoa to the skillet with the vegetable mixture and stir until everything is evenly mixed.

Spoon the quinoa mixture into the halved bell peppers, pressing down gently to pack the filling.

If using, sprinkle the shredded vegan cheese on top of each stuffed bell pepper.

Cover the baking dish with aluminum foil and bake in the preheated oven for 25-30 minutes, or until the bell peppers are tender.

Remove the foil and bake for an additional 5-10 minutes, or until the cheese is melted and bubbly (if using).

Remove from the oven and let cool for a few minutes before serving.

Garnish with fresh cilantro or parsley before serving, if desired. Enjoy these nutritious and flavorful Quinoa Stuffed Bell Peppers as a satisfying meal!

Shrimp Scampi Linguine

Ingredients:

- 12 ounces linguine pasta
- 1 pound large shrimp, peeled and deveined
- 4 tablespoons unsalted butter
- 4 tablespoons olive oil
- 4 cloves garlic, minced
- 1/4 teaspoon red pepper flakes (adjust to taste)
- 1/4 cup dry white wine
- Juice of 1 lemon
- Zest of 1 lemon
- Salt and black pepper to taste
- 1/4 cup chopped fresh parsley
- Grated Parmesan cheese for serving (optional)
- Lemon wedges for serving

Instructions:

Cook the linguine pasta according to the package instructions until al dente. Drain and set aside, reserving about 1/2 cup of pasta water.

In a large skillet, heat 2 tablespoons of butter and 2 tablespoons of olive oil over medium heat. Add the minced garlic and red pepper flakes, and sauté for 1-2 minutes until fragrant.

Add the shrimp to the skillet in a single layer. Cook for 2-3 minutes on each side until they turn pink and opaque. Remove the shrimp from the skillet and set aside.

In the same skillet, add the remaining butter and olive oil. Pour in the white wine, lemon juice, and lemon zest, stirring to combine. Let the sauce simmer for 2-3 minutes to reduce slightly.

Return the cooked shrimp to the skillet and toss to coat them evenly with the sauce. Season with salt and black pepper to taste.

Add the cooked linguine pasta to the skillet, tossing well to coat it with the sauce. If the sauce seems too thick, you can add some of the reserved pasta water to loosen it up.

Stir in the chopped fresh parsley and toss to combine.

Serve the Shrimp Scampi Linguine hot, garnished with grated Parmesan cheese if desired, and lemon wedges on the side for squeezing over the pasta. Enjoy this flavorful and satisfying dish!

Pan-Seared Tuna Steak with Mango Salsa

Ingredients:

For the Tuna Steak:

- 2 tuna steaks, about 6-8 ounces each
- 2 tablespoons soy sauce (or tamari for gluten-free)
- 1 tablespoon olive oil
- 1 teaspoon sesame oil
- 1 teaspoon grated fresh ginger
- 1 clove garlic, minced
- Salt and pepper to taste
- 1 tablespoon sesame seeds (optional, for garnish)
- Fresh cilantro or parsley for garnish

For the Mango Salsa:

- 1 ripe mango, peeled, pitted, and diced
- 1/2 red bell pepper, diced
- 1/4 cup red onion, finely chopped
- 1 jalapeño pepper, seeded and finely chopped
- Juice of 1 lime
- 2 tablespoons chopped fresh cilantro
- Salt and pepper to taste

Instructions:

In a shallow dish, whisk together the soy sauce, olive oil, sesame oil, grated ginger, minced garlic, salt, and pepper. Place the tuna steaks in the marinade, turning to coat evenly. Let marinate for at least 15-20 minutes at room temperature, or refrigerate for up to 1 hour.

While the tuna is marinating, prepare the mango salsa. In a bowl, combine the diced mango, red bell pepper, red onion, jalapeño pepper, lime juice, chopped cilantro, salt, and pepper. Stir well to combine, then cover and refrigerate until ready to serve.

Heat a large skillet over medium-high heat. Remove the tuna steaks from the marinade, shaking off any excess, and discard the remaining marinade.

Once the skillet is hot, add the tuna steaks and sear for 1-2 minutes on each side for rare to medium-rare doneness, depending on the thickness of the steaks. Be careful not to overcook.

Remove the tuna steaks from the skillet and let them rest for a few minutes before slicing.

To serve, slice the tuna steaks against the grain into thin slices. Arrange the slices on a serving platter or individual plates.

Spoon the mango salsa over the sliced tuna steaks. Sprinkle with sesame seeds and garnish with fresh cilantro or parsley.

Serve the Pan-Seared Tuna Steak with Mango Salsa immediately, accompanied by your favorite side dishes. Enjoy the vibrant flavors and textures of this delicious dish!

Chicken Caesar Salad with Avocado Dressing

Ingredients:

For the Avocado Dressing:

- 1 ripe avocado, peeled and pitted
- 1/4 cup plain Greek yogurt
- 2 tablespoons fresh lemon juice
- 2 tablespoons olive oil
- 1 clove garlic, minced
- 2 tablespoons grated Parmesan cheese
- Salt and pepper to taste
- Water (as needed to adjust consistency)

For the Salad:

- 2 boneless, skinless chicken breasts
- Salt and pepper to taste
- 1 tablespoon olive oil
- 1 head romaine lettuce, chopped
- 1 cup cherry tomatoes, halved
- 1/2 cup croutons
- 1/4 cup grated Parmesan cheese
- Optional: Anchovies for garnish (optional)

Instructions:

Preheat the grill or grill pan over medium-high heat.
Season the chicken breasts with salt and pepper on both sides.
Drizzle the olive oil over the chicken breasts, rubbing to coat evenly.
Grill the chicken breasts for 6-7 minutes per side, or until cooked through and no longer pink in the center. Remove from the grill and let rest for a few minutes before slicing.
While the chicken is grilling, prepare the avocado dressing. In a blender or food processor, combine the avocado, Greek yogurt, lemon juice, olive oil, minced garlic, grated Parmesan cheese, salt, and pepper. Blend until smooth and creamy.

If the dressing is too thick, you can thin it out with a little water until you reach your desired consistency.
In a large salad bowl, combine the chopped romaine lettuce, cherry tomatoes, and croutons.
Add the sliced grilled chicken to the salad.
Drizzle the avocado dressing over the salad, tossing gently to coat everything evenly.
Sprinkle the grated Parmesan cheese over the top of the salad.
If desired, garnish with anchovies.
Serve the Chicken Caesar Salad with Avocado Dressing immediately, and enjoy the delicious combination of flavors and textures!

Beef Wellington with Red Wine Reduction

Ingredients:

For the Beef Wellington:

- 1 1/2 to 2 pounds beef tenderloin
- Salt and pepper to taste
- 2 tablespoons olive oil
- 2 tablespoons Dijon mustard
- 1 package puff pastry, thawed according to package instructions
- 1 egg, beaten (for egg wash)

For the Mushroom Duxelles:

- 2 tablespoons unsalted butter
- 1 tablespoon olive oil
- 1 pound mushrooms (such as cremini or button), finely chopped
- 2 cloves garlic, minced
- 2 tablespoons chopped fresh thyme
- Salt and pepper to taste

For the Red Wine Reduction:

- 1 cup red wine
- 1/2 cup beef broth
- 2 tablespoons unsalted butter
- Salt and pepper to taste

Instructions:

Preheat the oven to 425°F (220°C).
Season the beef tenderloin generously with salt and pepper on all sides.
Heat the olive oil in a large skillet over high heat. Sear the beef tenderloin on all sides until browned, about 2 minutes per side. Remove from heat and let cool slightly.
Brush the seared beef tenderloin with Dijon mustard on all sides. Set aside.

To make the mushroom duxelles, heat the butter and olive oil in a skillet over medium heat. Add the chopped mushrooms and cook until they release their moisture and become golden brown, about 10-12 minutes.

Add the minced garlic and chopped fresh thyme to the skillet with the mushrooms. Cook for an additional 2-3 minutes. Season with salt and pepper to taste. Remove from heat and let cool slightly.

Roll out the puff pastry on a lightly floured surface into a large rectangle. Spread the mushroom duxelles evenly over the puff pastry.

Place the beef tenderloin in the center of the puff pastry, on top of the mushroom duxelles.

Wrap the puff pastry around the beef tenderloin, sealing the edges tightly. Trim any excess pastry if needed.

Brush the beaten egg over the top and sides of the puff pastry.

Place the Beef Wellington on a baking sheet lined with parchment paper.

Bake in the preheated oven for 35-40 minutes, or until the puff pastry is golden brown and the beef reaches your desired level of doneness. For medium-rare, the internal temperature should register 130-135°F (55-57°C) on a meat thermometer.

While the Beef Wellington is baking, prepare the red wine reduction. In a small saucepan, combine the red wine and beef broth. Bring to a simmer over medium heat and cook until reduced by half, about 10-12 minutes.

Remove the saucepan from heat and stir in the unsalted butter until melted. Season with salt and pepper to taste.

Once the Beef Wellington is done baking, let it rest for a few minutes before slicing.

Serve the Beef Wellington with the red wine reduction drizzled over the top. Enjoy this elegant and delicious dish!

Caprese Panini with Balsamic Glaze

Ingredients:

- 4 ciabatta rolls or sandwich bread of your choice
- 2 large tomatoes, sliced
- 1 ball fresh mozzarella cheese, sliced
- 1/4 cup fresh basil leaves
- 2 tablespoons balsamic glaze
- 2 tablespoons olive oil
- Salt and pepper to taste

Instructions:

Preheat a panini press or grill pan over medium heat.
Slice the ciabatta rolls in half horizontally to create the top and bottom halves of each sandwich.
Drizzle the bottom half of each ciabatta roll with olive oil.
Layer the sliced tomatoes, fresh mozzarella cheese, and basil leaves on the bottom halves of the ciabatta rolls. Season with salt and pepper to taste.
Drizzle the balsamic glaze over the tomato and mozzarella layers.
Place the top halves of the ciabatta rolls over the filling to form sandwiches.
Brush the outsides of the sandwiches with olive oil.
Place the sandwiches on the preheated panini press or grill pan.
Cook for 3-4 minutes, or until the bread is golden brown and the cheese is melted.
Carefully remove the sandwiches from the panini press or grill pan.
Let the sandwiches cool for a minute or two before slicing them in half.
Serve the Caprese Panini with Balsamic Glaze immediately. Enjoy this delicious and satisfying sandwich!

Seafood Paella

Ingredients:

- 1 1/2 cups Arborio rice (short-grain rice)
- 4 cups seafood or chicken broth
- 1 onion, finely chopped
- 3 cloves garlic, minced
- 1 red bell pepper, diced
- 1 yellow bell pepper, diced
- 1 tomato, diced
- 1/2 cup frozen peas
- 1/2 cup white wine (optional)
- 1 teaspoon smoked paprika
- 1/2 teaspoon saffron threads
- Salt and pepper to taste
- 1 pound mixed seafood (such as shrimp, mussels, squid, and/or clams), cleaned and prepared
- 1/4 cup chopped fresh parsley
- Lemon wedges for serving

Instructions:

In a small bowl, combine the saffron threads with a tablespoon of warm water and let it steep for 10-15 minutes.

In a large paella pan or skillet, heat some olive oil over medium heat. Add the chopped onion and garlic, and sauté until softened, about 3-4 minutes.

Add the diced bell peppers and tomato to the pan, and cook for another 3-4 minutes until the vegetables are tender.

Stir in the Arborio rice, smoked paprika, and saffron threads (with the water). Cook for 1-2 minutes, stirring constantly, until the rice is well coated with the spices.

Pour in the white wine (if using) and cook until it has mostly evaporated, about 2 minutes.

Gradually add the seafood or chicken broth to the pan, one cup at a time, stirring occasionally. Allow the rice to absorb most of the liquid before adding more broth. Cook for about 15-20 minutes, or until the rice is almost cooked through and most of the liquid has been absorbed.

Gently nestle the mixed seafood into the partially cooked rice, distributing it evenly across the pan. Arrange the mussels or clams hinge-side down, pressing them into the rice slightly.

Scatter the frozen peas over the top of the paella. Cover the pan with a lid or aluminum foil and continue to cook for another 5-10 minutes, or until the seafood is cooked through and the rice is tender.

Remove the lid and let the paella rest for a few minutes before serving.

Garnish with chopped fresh parsley and serve the Seafood Paella hot, with lemon wedges on the side for squeezing over the paella. Enjoy this flavorful and aromatic Spanish dish!

Thai Beef Salad with Peanut Dressing

Ingredients:

For the Salad:

- 1 lb beef steak (such as flank or sirloin), thinly sliced
- 8 cups mixed salad greens (such as lettuce, spinach, or arugula)
- 1 cucumber, thinly sliced
- 1 red bell pepper, thinly sliced
- 1 carrot, shredded
- 1/4 cup chopped fresh cilantro
- 1/4 cup chopped fresh mint
- 1/4 cup chopped roasted peanuts
- Lime wedges for serving

For the Peanut Dressing:

- 1/4 cup creamy peanut butter
- 2 tablespoons soy sauce
- 2 tablespoons lime juice
- 1 tablespoon rice vinegar
- 1 tablespoon honey or maple syrup
- 1 tablespoon sesame oil
- 2 cloves garlic, minced
- 1 teaspoon grated fresh ginger
- 1/4 teaspoon red pepper flakes (optional)
- 2-3 tablespoons water (as needed to adjust consistency)

Instructions:

In a bowl, combine all the ingredients for the peanut dressing: peanut butter, soy sauce, lime juice, rice vinegar, honey or maple syrup, sesame oil, minced garlic, grated ginger, and red pepper flakes (if using). Whisk until smooth. If the dressing is too thick, add water, one tablespoon at a time, until you reach your desired consistency. Set aside.

Heat a grill or grill pan over medium-high heat. Season the thinly sliced beef steak with salt and pepper.

Grill the beef steak for 2-3 minutes per side, or until cooked to your desired level of doneness. Remove from heat and let rest for a few minutes before slicing thinly against the grain.

In a large bowl, combine the mixed salad greens, sliced cucumber, sliced red bell pepper, shredded carrot, chopped cilantro, and chopped mint.

Add the sliced grilled beef steak to the salad bowl.

Drizzle the peanut dressing over the salad and toss gently to coat everything evenly.

Sprinkle the chopped roasted peanuts over the salad as a garnish.

Serve the Thai Beef Salad with Peanut Dressing immediately, with lime wedges on the side for squeezing over the salad. Enjoy this refreshing and flavorful salad!

Lobster Bisque Soup

Ingredients:

- 2 lobster tails (about 8 ounces each)
- 4 tablespoons unsalted butter
- 1/2 cup diced onion
- 1/4 cup diced celery
- 1/4 cup diced carrot
- 2 cloves garlic, minced
- 2 tablespoons tomato paste
- 1/4 cup all-purpose flour
- 4 cups seafood stock or chicken broth
- 1 cup heavy cream
- 1/4 cup dry sherry (optional)
- 1 bay leaf
- 1/4 teaspoon paprika
- Salt and pepper to taste
- Chopped fresh chives or parsley for garnish

Instructions:

Using kitchen shears, carefully cut down the center of each lobster tail shell, then remove the meat. Chop the lobster meat into small pieces and set aside. Reserve the shells for later.

In a large pot or Dutch oven, melt the butter over medium heat. Add the diced onion, celery, and carrot, and cook until softened, about 5-7 minutes.

Add the minced garlic and tomato paste to the pot, and cook for an additional 1-2 minutes, stirring constantly.

Sprinkle the flour over the vegetables and cook, stirring continuously, for 2-3 minutes to make a roux.

Gradually pour in the seafood stock or chicken broth, stirring constantly to avoid lumps. Add the bay leaf and paprika. Bring the mixture to a simmer and cook for 10-15 minutes, allowing the flavors to meld and the soup to thicken slightly.

Meanwhile, in a separate small saucepan, heat the heavy cream over low heat until warmed through.

Once the soup has simmered and thickened, remove the bay leaf. Use an immersion blender or transfer the soup in batches to a blender to puree until smooth.

Return the pureed soup to the pot. Stir in the warmed heavy cream and dry sherry (if using). Season with salt and pepper to taste.

Add the chopped lobster meat to the soup and simmer for 3-4 minutes, or until the lobster is cooked through and tender.

Ladle the Lobster Bisque Soup into bowls and garnish with chopped fresh chives or parsley.

Serve the Lobster Bisque Soup hot, accompanied by crusty bread or oyster crackers if desired. Enjoy this luxurious and comforting soup!

Spinach and Feta Stuffed Chicken Breast

Ingredients:

- 4 boneless, skinless chicken breasts
- Salt and pepper to taste
- 2 cups fresh spinach leaves
- 1/2 cup crumbled feta cheese
- 2 cloves garlic, minced
- 1 tablespoon olive oil
- 1 tablespoon Italian seasoning
- 1/4 cup grated Parmesan cheese
- Toothpicks or kitchen twine (optional)

Instructions:

Preheat your oven to 375°F (190°C).
Use a sharp knife to make a horizontal slit along the side of each chicken breast to create a pocket, being careful not to cut all the way through. Season the inside and outside of the chicken breasts with salt and pepper.
In a skillet, heat the olive oil over medium heat. Add the minced garlic and cook for 1 minute until fragrant.
Add the fresh spinach leaves to the skillet and cook until wilted, about 2-3 minutes. Remove from heat and let cool slightly.
Once cooled, mix the wilted spinach with the crumbled feta cheese.
Stuff each chicken breast with the spinach and feta mixture, dividing it evenly among the breasts. Secure the openings with toothpicks or kitchen twine, if necessary.
Place the stuffed chicken breasts in a baking dish. Drizzle with olive oil and sprinkle with Italian seasoning and grated Parmesan cheese.
Bake in the preheated oven for 25-30 minutes, or until the chicken is cooked through and reaches an internal temperature of 165°F (74°C).
Once cooked, remove the stuffed chicken breasts from the oven and let them rest for a few minutes before serving.
Serve the Spinach and Feta Stuffed Chicken Breast hot, garnished with additional Parmesan cheese and fresh herbs if desired. Enjoy this flavorful and satisfying dish!

Crab Cakes with Remoulade Sauce

Ingredients:

For the Crab Cakes:

- 1 pound lump crab meat, picked over for shells
- 1/2 cup breadcrumbs
- 1/4 cup mayonnaise
- 2 tablespoons Dijon mustard
- 2 green onions, finely chopped
- 1 tablespoon chopped fresh parsley
- 1 tablespoon lemon juice
- 1 teaspoon Worcestershire sauce
- 1/2 teaspoon Old Bay seasoning
- Salt and pepper to taste
- 2 tablespoons olive oil, for frying

For the Remoulade Sauce:

- 1/2 cup mayonnaise
- 2 tablespoons Dijon mustard
- 1 tablespoon chopped fresh parsley
- 1 tablespoon chopped green onion
- 1 tablespoon capers, chopped
- 1 tablespoon lemon juice
- 1 teaspoon hot sauce (such as Tabasco)
- 1/2 teaspoon paprika
- Salt and pepper to taste

Instructions:

In a large bowl, combine the lump crab meat, breadcrumbs, mayonnaise, Dijon mustard, chopped green onions, chopped parsley, lemon juice, Worcestershire sauce, Old Bay seasoning, salt, and pepper. Gently mix until well combined.

Form the crab mixture into 8 evenly-sized crab cakes, using your hands to shape them into patties. Place them on a baking sheet lined with parchment paper and refrigerate for 30 minutes to firm up.

While the crab cakes are chilling, prepare the remoulade sauce. In a small bowl, combine the mayonnaise, Dijon mustard, chopped parsley, chopped green onion, capers, lemon juice, hot sauce, paprika, salt, and pepper. Stir until well combined. Cover and refrigerate until ready to serve.

Heat the olive oil in a large skillet over medium-high heat. Once hot, carefully add the crab cakes to the skillet, working in batches if necessary to avoid overcrowding the pan.

Cook the crab cakes for 3-4 minutes on each side, or until golden brown and heated through. Use a spatula to carefully flip them halfway through cooking.

Once the crab cakes are cooked, transfer them to a serving platter or individual plates.

Serve the Crab Cakes with Remoulade Sauce on the side for dipping, along with lemon wedges if desired. Enjoy these delicious and flavorful crab cakes as a appetizer or main course!

Mediterranean Veggie Wrap with Hummus

Ingredients:

For the Hummus:

- 1 (15-ounce) can chickpeas (garbanzo beans), drained and rinsed
- 1/4 cup tahini
- 2 cloves garlic, minced
- 3 tablespoons fresh lemon juice
- 2 tablespoons olive oil
- 1/2 teaspoon ground cumin
- Salt to taste
- 2-4 tablespoons water, as needed

For the Wrap:

- 4 large whole wheat or spinach tortillas
- 1 cup hummus (store-bought or homemade)
- 2 cups mixed salad greens (such as lettuce or spinach)
- 1 cucumber, thinly sliced
- 1 bell pepper, thinly sliced
- 1/2 red onion, thinly sliced
- 1/2 cup sliced Kalamata olives
- 1/4 cup crumbled feta cheese (optional)
- Fresh parsley or cilantro for garnish (optional)

Instructions:

To make the hummus, combine the chickpeas, tahini, minced garlic, lemon juice, olive oil, ground cumin, and salt in a food processor. Blend until smooth, adding water as needed to achieve your desired consistency. Taste and adjust seasoning as necessary. Set aside.

Lay out the tortillas on a clean work surface.

Spread about 1/4 cup of hummus onto each tortilla, leaving a border around the edges.

Divide the mixed salad greens evenly among the tortillas, arranging them in a line down the center of each wrap.

Top the salad greens with sliced cucumber, bell pepper, red onion, and Kalamata olives.

If using, sprinkle crumbled feta cheese over the veggies.

Roll up the wraps tightly, folding in the sides as you go, to enclose the filling.

If desired, slice the wraps in half diagonally for easier eating.

Garnish the Mediterranean Veggie Wraps with fresh parsley or cilantro, if desired.

Serve immediately, or wrap tightly in plastic wrap or aluminum foil for an on-the-go meal or packed lunch. Enjoy these flavorful and nutritious wraps filled with Mediterranean-inspired ingredients!

Steak Fajita Bowl with Guacamole

Ingredients:

For the Steak Fajitas:

- 1 lb flank steak, skirt steak, or sirloin steak
- 2 tablespoons olive oil
- 1 tablespoon lime juice
- 2 cloves garlic, minced
- 1 teaspoon chili powder
- 1 teaspoon ground cumin
- 1 teaspoon smoked paprika
- Salt and pepper to taste
- 1 onion, thinly sliced
- 1 bell pepper (any color), thinly sliced

For the Guacamole:

- 2 ripe avocados
- 1 small tomato, diced
- 1/4 cup finely chopped red onion
- 1/4 cup chopped fresh cilantro
- 1 tablespoon lime juice
- Salt and pepper to taste

For Serving:

- Cooked rice or cauliflower rice
- Black beans, drained and rinsed
- Shredded lettuce or mixed greens
- Sour cream or Greek yogurt (optional)
- Sliced jalapeños (optional)
- Lime wedges (optional)

Instructions:

In a small bowl, whisk together the olive oil, lime juice, minced garlic, chili powder, ground cumin, smoked paprika, salt, and pepper to make the marinade.

Place the steak in a shallow dish or resealable plastic bag, and pour the marinade over the steak. Make sure the steak is well coated in the marinade. Cover or seal the dish/bag and let the steak marinate in the refrigerator for at least 30 minutes, or up to 4 hours.

While the steak is marinating, prepare the guacamole. Cut the avocados in half and remove the pits. Scoop the avocado flesh into a bowl and mash with a fork until smooth or slightly chunky, depending on your preference. Stir in the diced tomato, chopped red onion, chopped cilantro, lime juice, salt, and pepper. Taste and adjust seasoning as needed. Cover the guacamole with plastic wrap, pressing it directly onto the surface to prevent browning, and refrigerate until ready to use.

Heat a grill or grill pan over medium-high heat. Remove the steak from the marinade and discard any excess marinade. Grill the steak for 4-5 minutes per side, or until cooked to your desired level of doneness. Remove the steak from the grill and let it rest for a few minutes before slicing thinly against the grain.

In a separate skillet, heat a tablespoon of olive oil over medium-high heat. Add the sliced onion and bell pepper to the skillet and cook, stirring occasionally, until softened and slightly charred, about 5-7 minutes.

To assemble the steak fajita bowls, divide the cooked rice or cauliflower rice among serving bowls. Top with the sliced steak, sautéed onion and bell pepper, black beans, shredded lettuce or mixed greens, and a generous scoop of guacamole.

If desired, garnish the bowls with sour cream or Greek yogurt, sliced jalapeños, and lime wedges.

Serve the Steak Fajita Bowls with Guacamole immediately, allowing everyone to customize their bowls with their favorite toppings. Enjoy this delicious and satisfying meal!

Vegetable Stir-Fry with Cashew Nuts

Ingredients:

For the Stir-Fry Sauce:

- 1/4 cup soy sauce (or tamari for gluten-free)
- 2 tablespoons hoisin sauce
- 1 tablespoon rice vinegar
- 1 tablespoon sesame oil
- 1 tablespoon honey or maple syrup
- 1 tablespoon cornstarch
- 1/4 cup water

For the Stir-Fry:

- 2 tablespoons vegetable oil
- 2 cloves garlic, minced
- 1 tablespoon grated fresh ginger
- 1 onion, thinly sliced
- 2 bell peppers (any color), thinly sliced
- 2 carrots, julienned or thinly sliced
- 1 cup snow peas, trimmed
- 1 cup broccoli florets
- 1/2 cup unsalted cashew nuts
- Cooked rice or noodles, for serving
- Chopped green onions and sesame seeds for garnish (optional)

Instructions:

In a small bowl, whisk together all the ingredients for the stir-fry sauce: soy sauce, hoisin sauce, rice vinegar, sesame oil, honey or maple syrup, cornstarch, and water. Set aside.
Heat the vegetable oil in a large skillet or wok over medium-high heat. Add the minced garlic and grated ginger, and stir-fry for 30 seconds, or until fragrant. Add the sliced onion to the skillet and stir-fry for 2-3 minutes, until softened.

Add the sliced bell peppers, julienned carrots, snow peas, and broccoli florets to the skillet. Stir-fry for 4-5 minutes, or until the vegetables are tender-crisp.

Pour the prepared stir-fry sauce over the vegetables in the skillet. Stir well to coat the vegetables evenly in the sauce.

Add the unsalted cashew nuts to the skillet and toss to combine with the vegetables and sauce.

Continue to cook for another 2-3 minutes, or until the sauce has thickened slightly and the cashews are heated through.

Remove the skillet from heat. Taste and adjust seasoning if necessary.

Serve the vegetable stir-fry with cashew nuts hot over cooked rice or noodles. Garnish with chopped green onions and sesame seeds, if desired.

Enjoy this flavorful and nutritious Vegetable Stir-Fry with Cashew Nuts as a delicious and satisfying meal!

Greek Orzo Salad with Lemon Vinaigrette

Ingredients:

For the Salad:

- 1 cup uncooked orzo pasta
- 1 cucumber, diced
- 1 pint cherry tomatoes, halved
- 1/2 red onion, thinly sliced
- 1/2 cup Kalamata olives, pitted and sliced
- 1/2 cup crumbled feta cheese
- 1/4 cup chopped fresh parsley
- 1/4 cup chopped fresh dill
- Salt and pepper to taste

For the Lemon Vinaigrette:

- 1/4 cup extra-virgin olive oil
- 2 tablespoons fresh lemon juice
- 1 teaspoon Dijon mustard
- 1 clove garlic, minced
- 1 teaspoon honey or maple syrup
- 1/2 teaspoon dried oregano
- Salt and pepper to taste

Instructions:

Cook the orzo pasta according to the package instructions until al dente. Drain and rinse the cooked orzo under cold water to cool it down. Transfer the orzo to a large mixing bowl.

Add the diced cucumber, halved cherry tomatoes, thinly sliced red onion, sliced Kalamata olives, crumbled feta cheese, chopped fresh parsley, and chopped fresh dill to the bowl with the cooked orzo.

In a small bowl or jar, whisk together the extra-virgin olive oil, fresh lemon juice, Dijon mustard, minced garlic, honey or maple syrup, dried oregano, salt, and pepper to make the lemon vinaigrette.

Pour the lemon vinaigrette over the salad ingredients in the large mixing bowl.
Toss the salad gently until all the ingredients are well coated in the dressing.
Taste and adjust seasoning as needed with salt and pepper.
Cover the bowl with plastic wrap and refrigerate the Greek Orzo Salad for at least 30 minutes to allow the flavors to meld.
Before serving, give the salad a final toss to redistribute the dressing and garnish with additional chopped fresh parsley or dill if desired.
Serve the Greek Orzo Salad with Lemon Vinaigrette chilled as a refreshing and flavorful side dish or light meal. Enjoy!

Pesto Chicken Sandwich with Sun-Dried Tomatoes

Ingredients:

For the Pesto Chicken:

- 2 boneless, skinless chicken breasts
- Salt and pepper to taste
- 2 tablespoons olive oil
- 1/4 cup prepared pesto sauce

For the Sandwich:

- 4 slices of bread (such as ciabatta, sourdough, or whole grain)
- 1/4 cup sun-dried tomatoes (packed in oil), drained and chopped
- 1/2 cup baby spinach leaves
- 4 slices mozzarella cheese or provolone cheese

Instructions:

Preheat your grill or grill pan over medium-high heat.
Season the chicken breasts with salt and pepper on both sides.
Drizzle the olive oil over the chicken breasts, rubbing to coat evenly.
Grill the chicken breasts for 6-7 minutes per side, or until cooked through and no longer pink in the center.
Once the chicken is cooked, remove it from the grill and let it rest for a few minutes. Then, slice the chicken breasts into thin slices.
To assemble the sandwiches, spread a tablespoon of pesto sauce onto each slice of bread.
Layer the sliced chicken onto two slices of bread.
Top the chicken with chopped sun-dried tomatoes and baby spinach leaves.
Place a slice of mozzarella or provolone cheese on top of the spinach.
Place the remaining slices of bread on top to form sandwiches.
If desired, lightly brush the outsides of the sandwiches with olive oil or butter.
Heat a skillet or panini press over medium heat. Once hot, add the sandwiches and cook for 3-4 minutes on each side, or until the bread is golden brown and the cheese is melted.

Remove the sandwiches from the skillet or panini press and let them cool for a minute before slicing.
Serve the Pesto Chicken Sandwiches with Sun-Dried Tomatoes immediately, and enjoy the delicious combination of flavors!

Teriyaki Salmon Bowl with Sesame Seeds

Ingredients:

For the Teriyaki Salmon:

- 4 salmon fillets (about 6 ounces each)
- 1/4 cup soy sauce
- 2 tablespoons mirin (Japanese sweet rice wine)
- 2 tablespoons honey or maple syrup
- 1 tablespoon rice vinegar
- 1 clove garlic, minced
- 1 teaspoon grated fresh ginger
- 1 teaspoon sesame oil
- 1 tablespoon cornstarch
- 2 tablespoons water
- Sesame seeds for garnish

For the Bowl:

- 2 cups cooked brown rice or sushi rice
- 2 cups mixed vegetables (such as broccoli florets, sliced bell peppers, shredded carrots, and snap peas)
- 1 tablespoon vegetable oil
- Salt and pepper to taste
- Sliced green onions for garnish
- Sliced avocado for garnish (optional)

Instructions:

Preheat your oven to 400°F (200°C). Line a baking sheet with parchment paper or foil for easy cleanup.
In a small saucepan, combine the soy sauce, mirin, honey or maple syrup, rice vinegar, minced garlic, grated ginger, and sesame oil. Bring the mixture to a simmer over medium heat.

In a separate small bowl, whisk together the cornstarch and water until smooth. Add the cornstarch slurry to the saucepan and whisk until the sauce thickens, about 1-2 minutes. Remove the sauce from heat and set aside.

Place the salmon fillets on the prepared baking sheet. Brush the tops of the salmon fillets with some of the prepared teriyaki sauce, reserving the rest for later.

Bake the salmon in the preheated oven for 12-15 minutes, or until the salmon is cooked through and flakes easily with a fork.

While the salmon is baking, heat the vegetable oil in a large skillet or wok over medium-high heat. Add the mixed vegetables to the skillet and stir-fry for 4-5 minutes, or until tender-crisp. Season with salt and pepper to taste.

To assemble the bowls, divide the cooked rice among serving bowls. Top each bowl with a portion of the stir-fried vegetables.

Place a teriyaki salmon fillet on top of the vegetables in each bowl.

Drizzle the remaining teriyaki sauce over the salmon fillets.

Sprinkle sesame seeds over the bowls for garnish, along with sliced green onions and sliced avocado if desired.

Serve the Teriyaki Salmon Bowls with Sesame Seeds hot, and enjoy this delicious and nutritious meal!

Roasted Butternut Squash Soup with Sage Croutons

Ingredients:

For the Roasted Butternut Squash Soup:

- 1 large butternut squash, peeled, seeded, and diced
- 1 onion, chopped
- 2 carrots, peeled and chopped
- 2 cloves garlic, minced
- 4 cups vegetable broth or chicken broth
- 1 teaspoon ground cinnamon
- 1/2 teaspoon ground nutmeg
- Salt and pepper to taste
- 2 tablespoons olive oil

For the Sage Croutons:

- 4 slices bread (such as baguette or ciabatta), cut into cubes
- 2 tablespoons olive oil
- 2 tablespoons chopped fresh sage
- Salt and pepper to taste

Instructions:

Preheat your oven to 400°F (200°C).

Place the diced butternut squash, chopped onion, chopped carrots, and minced garlic on a large baking sheet. Drizzle with olive oil and season with salt, pepper, ground cinnamon, and ground nutmeg. Toss to coat evenly.

Roast the vegetables in the preheated oven for 25-30 minutes, or until they are tender and lightly caramelized.

While the vegetables are roasting, prepare the sage croutons. In a bowl, toss the bread cubes with olive oil, chopped fresh sage, salt, and pepper until evenly coated. Spread the seasoned bread cubes on a baking sheet in a single layer.

Bake the sage croutons in the preheated oven for 10-12 minutes, or until golden brown and crispy. Remove from the oven and set aside.

Once the roasted vegetables are done, transfer them to a large pot. Add the vegetable broth or chicken broth to the pot.

Use an immersion blender to blend the soup until smooth and creamy. Alternatively, you can transfer the soup in batches to a blender and blend until smooth, then return it to the pot.

Place the pot of blended soup over medium heat. Bring to a simmer and cook for an additional 5-10 minutes to allow the flavors to meld.

Taste the soup and adjust seasoning with salt and pepper as needed.

Ladle the Roasted Butternut Squash Soup into bowls and garnish with the sage croutons.

Serve the soup hot, and enjoy the comforting flavors of roasted butternut squash with the crispy sage croutons!

Pan-Seared Scallops with Lemon Butter Sauce

Ingredients:

For the Scallops:

- 1 pound large sea scallops, side muscle removed
- Salt and pepper to taste
- 2 tablespoons olive oil
- 2 tablespoons unsalted butter

For the Lemon Butter Sauce:

- 1/4 cup dry white wine
- 2 tablespoons fresh lemon juice
- 2 cloves garlic, minced
- 4 tablespoons unsalted butter, cold and cubed
- 1 tablespoon chopped fresh parsley
- Salt and pepper to taste
- Lemon wedges for serving

Instructions:

Pat the scallops dry with paper towels and season both sides generously with salt and pepper.
Heat the olive oil in a large skillet over medium-high heat until shimmering but not smoking.
Carefully add the scallops to the skillet in a single layer, making sure they are not touching each other. Cook undisturbed for 2-3 minutes, or until a golden crust forms on the bottom.
Flip the scallops over and add the butter to the skillet. Cook for an additional 2-3 minutes, basting the scallops with the melted butter, until they are cooked through and opaque in the center.
Transfer the cooked scallops to a plate and cover loosely with foil to keep warm.
In the same skillet, add the white wine, lemon juice, and minced garlic. Bring to a simmer over medium heat, scraping up any browned bits from the bottom of the skillet.

Let the sauce reduce for 1-2 minutes, then reduce the heat to low.

Gradually add the cold cubed butter to the skillet, a few pieces at a time, whisking constantly until the butter is melted and the sauce is smooth and slightly thickened.

Stir in the chopped fresh parsley and season the sauce with salt and pepper to taste.

Return the cooked scallops to the skillet and gently toss them in the lemon butter sauce to coat.

Remove the skillet from heat and transfer the scallops and sauce to a serving platter.

Serve the Pan-Seared Scallops with Lemon Butter Sauce hot, garnished with lemon wedges for squeezing over the scallops if desired.

Enjoy these elegant and flavorful scallops as a delicious appetizer or main course!

Ratatouille with Garlic Crostini

Ingredients:

For the Ratatouille:

- 1 eggplant, diced
- 2 zucchini, diced
- 1 yellow bell pepper, diced
- 1 red bell pepper, diced
- 1 onion, diced
- 3 cloves garlic, minced
- 2 cups diced tomatoes (canned or fresh)
- 2 tablespoons tomato paste
- 2 tablespoons olive oil
- 1 teaspoon dried thyme
- 1 teaspoon dried oregano
- Salt and pepper to taste
- Fresh basil leaves for garnish

For the Garlic Crostini:

- Baguette or French bread, sliced into 1/2-inch thick slices
- 2 tablespoons olive oil
- 2 cloves garlic, peeled and halved

Instructions:

Preheat your oven to 375°F (190°C).

In a large skillet or Dutch oven, heat the olive oil over medium heat. Add the diced eggplant, zucchini, yellow bell pepper, red bell pepper, onion, and minced garlic to the skillet. Cook, stirring occasionally, for 5-7 minutes, or until the vegetables are slightly softened.

Add the diced tomatoes, tomato paste, dried thyme, dried oregano, salt, and pepper to the skillet. Stir to combine.

Cover the skillet and let the ratatouille simmer over low heat for 20-25 minutes, stirring occasionally, until the vegetables are tender and the flavors have melded together.

While the ratatouille is simmering, prepare the garlic crostini. Place the bread slices on a baking sheet in a single layer. Drizzle with olive oil and rub each slice with the halved garlic cloves.

Bake the garlic crostini in the preheated oven for 8-10 minutes, or until golden and crisp.

Once the ratatouille is ready, taste and adjust seasoning as needed with salt and pepper.

Serve the ratatouille hot, garnished with fresh basil leaves, alongside the garlic crostini.

Enjoy this classic French dish of Ratatouille with Garlic Crostini as a flavorful and satisfying meal!

BBQ Pulled Pork Sandwich with Coleslaw

Ingredients:

For the BBQ Pulled Pork:

- 3-4 pounds pork shoulder or pork butt
- Salt and pepper to taste
- 1 tablespoon olive oil
- 1 onion, chopped
- 3 cloves garlic, minced
- 1 cup BBQ sauce (store-bought or homemade)
- 1 cup chicken broth or water

For the Coleslaw:

- 4 cups shredded cabbage (green or a mix of green and purple)
- 1 carrot, grated
- 1/2 cup mayonnaise
- 2 tablespoons apple cider vinegar
- 1 tablespoon honey or maple syrup
- Salt and pepper to taste

For Serving:

- Sandwich rolls or buns
- Additional BBQ sauce for serving (optional)
- Pickles (optional)

Instructions:

Season the pork shoulder or pork butt generously with salt and pepper on all sides.

Heat the olive oil in a large skillet or Dutch oven over medium-high heat. Add the chopped onion and minced garlic to the skillet and cook until softened and fragrant, about 3-4 minutes.

Add the seasoned pork shoulder or pork butt to the skillet and sear on all sides until browned, about 3-4 minutes per side.

Transfer the seared pork to a slow cooker. Pour the BBQ sauce and chicken broth or water over the pork.

Cover and cook on low heat for 8-10 hours or on high heat for 4-6 hours, or until the pork is tender and easily shreds with a fork.

While the pork is cooking, prepare the coleslaw. In a large bowl, combine the shredded cabbage and grated carrot.

In a separate small bowl, whisk together the mayonnaise, apple cider vinegar, honey or maple syrup, salt, and pepper to make the coleslaw dressing.

Pour the dressing over the cabbage mixture and toss until well coated. Cover and refrigerate the coleslaw until ready to serve.

Once the pork is done cooking, use two forks to shred the meat in the slow cooker. Mix the shredded pork with the BBQ sauce and juices in the slow cooker.

To assemble the sandwiches, place a generous amount of BBQ pulled pork on the bottom half of each sandwich roll or bun.

Top the pulled pork with a spoonful of coleslaw.

If desired, drizzle extra BBQ sauce over the coleslaw and top with pickles.

Place the top half of the sandwich roll or bun on top.

Serve the BBQ Pulled Pork Sandwiches with Coleslaw hot and enjoy this delicious and comforting meal!

Sushi Burrito with Spicy Mayo

Ingredients:

For the Sushi Burrito:

- 4 nori seaweed sheets
- 2 cups sushi rice, cooked and seasoned with rice vinegar
- 1/2 pound sushi-grade raw fish (such as tuna or salmon), thinly sliced
- 1 cucumber, julienned
- 1 avocado, sliced
- 1/2 cup shredded carrots
- 1/2 cup shredded cabbage
- 1/4 cup pickled ginger
- Soy sauce, for serving

For the Spicy Mayo:

- 1/4 cup mayonnaise
- 1 tablespoon Sriracha sauce (adjust to taste)
- 1 teaspoon rice vinegar
- 1/2 teaspoon sesame oil
- Salt to taste

Instructions:

In a small bowl, combine all the ingredients for the spicy mayo: mayonnaise, Sriracha sauce, rice vinegar, sesame oil, and salt. Stir until well combined. Adjust the amount of Sriracha sauce to your desired level of spiciness. Set aside.

Lay a nori seaweed sheet on a clean surface, with the shiny side facing down. Spread a layer of cooked and seasoned sushi rice evenly over the nori sheet, leaving a small border along the edges.

Arrange the sliced raw fish, julienned cucumber, sliced avocado, shredded carrots, shredded cabbage, and pickled ginger in the center of the rice.

Drizzle the spicy mayo over the fillings.

To roll the sushi burrito, fold the bottom edge of the nori sheet over the fillings, using a bamboo sushi rolling mat to help tuck and roll tightly.

Continue rolling the sushi burrito until it forms a tight cylinder, sealing the edge of the nori sheet with a bit of water to help it stick.

Use a sharp knife to slice the sushi burrito in half or into smaller pieces, if desired.

Serve the Sushi Burrito with Spicy Mayo with soy sauce for dipping.

Enjoy this unique fusion dish that combines the flavors of sushi with the convenience of a burrito!

Mushroom Risotto with Parmesan Crisps

Ingredients:

For the Mushroom Risotto:

- 1 cup Arborio rice
- 4 cups chicken or vegetable broth
- 2 tablespoons olive oil
- 1 onion, finely chopped
- 2 cloves garlic, minced
- 8 ounces mushrooms (such as cremini or shiitake), sliced
- 1/2 cup dry white wine
- 1/2 cup grated Parmesan cheese
- Salt and pepper to taste
- Fresh parsley, chopped, for garnish

For the Parmesan Crisps:

- 1 cup grated Parmesan cheese

Instructions:

In a saucepan, heat the chicken or vegetable broth over medium heat. Keep it warm while preparing the risotto.

In a separate large skillet or saucepan, heat the olive oil over medium heat. Add the finely chopped onion and minced garlic, and cook until softened, about 3-4 minutes.

Add the sliced mushrooms to the skillet and cook until they release their moisture and become tender, about 5-6 minutes.

Stir in the Arborio rice and cook for 1-2 minutes, stirring constantly, until the rice is lightly toasted.

Pour in the dry white wine and cook, stirring frequently, until the wine has evaporated.

Begin adding the warm chicken or vegetable broth to the rice mixture, one ladleful at a time, stirring constantly and allowing the liquid to be absorbed before adding more. Continue this process until the rice is creamy and tender, about 20-25 minutes.

Stir in the grated Parmesan cheese until melted and well combined. Season the risotto with salt and pepper to taste.

While the risotto is cooking, preheat your oven to 400°F (200°C) and line a baking sheet with parchment paper.

To make the Parmesan crisps, evenly distribute the grated Parmesan cheese into 8 small piles on the prepared baking sheet, leaving space between each pile.

Bake the Parmesan crisps in the preheated oven for 5-7 minutes, or until they are golden and crispy. Remove from the oven and let them cool slightly.

Once the risotto is ready, divide it among serving bowls and garnish with chopped fresh parsley.

Serve the Mushroom Risotto with Parmesan Crisps alongside or on top of each bowl of risotto.

Enjoy this creamy and flavorful risotto dish, topped with crunchy Parmesan crisps for added texture and richness!

Tofu Buddha Bowl with Tahini Dressing

Ingredients:

For the Tofu:

- 14 oz (400g) firm tofu, drained and pressed
- 2 tablespoons soy sauce
- 1 tablespoon olive oil
- 1 teaspoon garlic powder
- 1 teaspoon paprika
- Salt and pepper to taste

For the Buddha Bowl:

- 2 cups cooked quinoa or brown rice
- 2 cups mixed greens (such as spinach, kale, or arugula)
- 1 cup cherry tomatoes, halved
- 1 cucumber, sliced
- 1 avocado, sliced
- 1/2 cup shredded carrots
- 1/4 cup sliced radishes
- 1/4 cup sliced almonds or sesame seeds for garnish

For the Tahini Dressing:

- 1/4 cup tahini
- 2 tablespoons lemon juice
- 2 tablespoons water
- 1 tablespoon maple syrup or honey
- 1 clove garlic, minced
- Salt and pepper to taste

Instructions:

Preheat your oven to 400°F (200°C).

Cut the pressed tofu into cubes or slices. In a bowl, whisk together the soy sauce, olive oil, garlic powder, paprika, salt, and pepper. Add the tofu cubes to the marinade and toss to coat evenly.

Place the marinated tofu on a baking sheet lined with parchment paper. Bake in the preheated oven for 20-25 minutes, flipping halfway through, until the tofu is golden brown and crispy.

While the tofu is baking, prepare the Buddha Bowl ingredients. Divide the cooked quinoa or brown rice, mixed greens, cherry tomatoes, cucumber slices, avocado slices, shredded carrots, and sliced radishes among serving bowls.

In a small bowl, whisk together the tahini, lemon juice, water, maple syrup or honey, minced garlic, salt, and pepper to make the tahini dressing. If the dressing is too thick, add more water to reach your desired consistency.

Once the tofu is done baking, remove it from the oven and let it cool slightly.

Add the baked tofu cubes to the Buddha Bowls.

Drizzle the tahini dressing over the Buddha Bowls.

Sprinkle sliced almonds or sesame seeds on top for garnish.

Serve the Tofu Buddha Bowls with Tahini Dressing immediately and enjoy this nutritious and flavorful meal!

Chicken Piccata with Capers

Ingredients:

For the Chicken:

- 4 boneless, skinless chicken breasts
- Salt and pepper to taste
- 1/2 cup all-purpose flour, for dredging
- 2 tablespoons olive oil
- 4 tablespoons unsalted butter

For the Piccata Sauce:

- 1/2 cup chicken broth
- 1/4 cup fresh lemon juice (about 2 lemons)
- 1/4 cup capers, drained
- 1/4 cup chopped fresh parsley
- 2 cloves garlic, minced

Instructions:

Start by pounding the chicken breasts to an even thickness between two sheets of plastic wrap or parchment paper. Season both sides of the chicken breasts with salt and pepper.
Dredge the chicken breasts in the all-purpose flour, shaking off any excess.
In a large skillet, heat the olive oil and 2 tablespoons of butter over medium-high heat. Once the butter has melted and the skillet is hot, add the chicken breasts to the skillet.
Cook the chicken breasts for 3-4 minutes on each side, or until they are golden brown and cooked through. Transfer the cooked chicken breasts to a plate and cover them loosely with foil to keep warm.
In the same skillet, add the chicken broth, lemon juice, capers, chopped fresh parsley, and minced garlic. Stir to combine, scraping up any browned bits from the bottom of the skillet.
Let the sauce simmer for 2-3 minutes, or until it has slightly thickened.

Add the remaining 2 tablespoons of butter to the skillet and stir until melted and incorporated into the sauce.

Return the cooked chicken breasts to the skillet, spooning the piccata sauce over them.

Cook the chicken breasts in the sauce for another 2-3 minutes, allowing the flavors to meld together.

Serve the Chicken Piccata with Capers hot, garnished with additional chopped parsley if desired.

Enjoy this classic Italian dish with its tangy and savory flavors! Serve it with your choice of side dishes such as pasta, rice, or vegetables.

Lobster Mac and Cheese

Ingredients:

- 8 oz (about 225g) elbow macaroni or pasta of your choice
- 2 lobster tails, cooked and meat removed from the shells, chopped into bite-sized pieces
- 2 tablespoons unsalted butter
- 2 tablespoons all-purpose flour
- 2 cups whole milk
- 2 cups shredded sharp cheddar cheese
- 1 cup shredded Gruyère cheese
- 1/2 teaspoon mustard powder
- Salt and pepper to taste
- 1/4 cup breadcrumbs (optional, for topping)
- Chopped fresh parsley for garnish

Instructions:

Preheat your oven to 375°F (190°C). Grease a 9x13-inch baking dish or individual ramekins if making individual servings.

Cook the elbow macaroni according to the package instructions until al dente. Drain and set aside.

In a large saucepan, melt the butter over medium heat. Add the flour and whisk constantly for about 1 minute to make a roux.

Slowly pour in the whole milk while whisking constantly to avoid lumps. Continue to cook and whisk until the mixture thickens, about 5-7 minutes.

Reduce the heat to low and stir in the shredded cheddar cheese and shredded Gruyère cheese until melted and smooth.

Stir in the mustard powder, salt, and pepper to taste.

Add the cooked macaroni and chopped lobster meat to the cheese sauce, stirring until everything is well coated.

Transfer the mac and cheese mixture to the prepared baking dish or individual ramekins, spreading it out evenly.

If desired, sprinkle breadcrumbs over the top of the mac and cheese for a crispy topping.

Bake in the preheated oven for 20-25 minutes, or until the cheese is bubbly and the top is golden brown.

Remove from the oven and let it cool slightly before serving.
Garnish with chopped fresh parsley before serving.
Serve the Lobster Mac and Cheese hot as a decadent and satisfying main dish or side dish. Enjoy!

Thai Green Curry with Tofu and Vegetables

Ingredients:

For the Thai Green Curry Paste:

- 2 stalks lemongrass, thinly sliced (outer tough layers removed)
- 4 green Thai chilies, chopped (adjust to taste)
- 4 cloves garlic, minced
- 1 small onion, chopped
- 1-inch piece of ginger, peeled and chopped
- 1 tablespoon chopped fresh cilantro stems
- 1 tablespoon chopped fresh basil leaves
- 1 tablespoon chopped fresh cilantro leaves
- 1 tablespoon chopped fresh kaffir lime leaves (optional)
- 1 tablespoon ground coriander
- 1 teaspoon ground cumin
- 1/2 teaspoon ground white pepper
- 1/2 teaspoon salt
- Zest of 1 lime
- Juice of 1 lime
- 2 tablespoons vegetable oil

For the Curry:

- 14 oz (400g) firm tofu, drained and cubed
- 2 tablespoons vegetable oil
- 1 can (13.5 oz / 400ml) coconut milk
- 1 cup vegetable broth
- 2 tablespoons soy sauce or tamari
- 2 tablespoons brown sugar or coconut sugar
- 2 cups mixed vegetables (such as bell peppers, carrots, zucchini, broccoli)
- Fresh Thai basil leaves for garnish (optional)
- Cooked rice for serving

Instructions:

Prepare the Thai Green Curry Paste: In a food processor or blender, combine all the ingredients for the curry paste. Blend until smooth, scraping down the sides as needed. If necessary, add a little water to help the blending process.

In a large skillet or wok, heat 2 tablespoons of vegetable oil over medium heat. Add the cubed tofu and cook until golden brown on all sides. Remove the tofu from the skillet and set aside.

In the same skillet, add another tablespoon of oil if needed. Add 3-4 tablespoons of the prepared Thai Green Curry Paste (or more if desired) and cook for 1-2 minutes, stirring constantly, until fragrant.

Pour in the coconut milk and vegetable broth, stirring to combine. Bring the mixture to a simmer.

Stir in the soy sauce or tamari and brown sugar or coconut sugar, adjusting the sweetness and saltiness to your taste.

Add the mixed vegetables to the skillet and simmer for 5-7 minutes, or until the vegetables are tender but still crisp.

Return the cooked tofu to the skillet and gently stir to combine with the curry sauce and vegetables. Simmer for another 2-3 minutes to heat through.

Taste the curry and adjust seasoning if needed, adding more salt, sugar, or curry paste as desired.

Remove the skillet from heat and serve the Thai Green Curry with Tofu and Vegetables hot, garnished with fresh Thai basil leaves if desired.

Serve over cooked rice and enjoy this flavorful and aromatic Thai dish!

Prosciutto-Wrapped Asparagus with Balsamic Glaze

Ingredients:

- 1 pound (450g) asparagus spears, tough ends trimmed
- 4-6 slices prosciutto, sliced thinly
- 1 tablespoon olive oil
- Salt and pepper to taste
- Balsamic glaze for drizzling

Instructions:

Preheat your oven to 400°F (200°C). Line a baking sheet with parchment paper or aluminum foil for easy cleanup.

Toss the trimmed asparagus spears with olive oil, salt, and pepper until evenly coated.

Divide the asparagus spears into bundles, depending on the size of your prosciutto slices. Typically, 3-4 asparagus spears per bundle work well.

Take a slice of prosciutto and wrap it tightly around each bundle of asparagus, starting from the bottom and working your way up to the tips. Repeat with the remaining asparagus spears and prosciutto slices.

Place the prosciutto-wrapped asparagus bundles on the prepared baking sheet, seam side down.

Bake in the preheated oven for 10-12 minutes, or until the asparagus is tender and the prosciutto is crispy.

Remove from the oven and let the prosciutto-wrapped asparagus cool slightly.

Drizzle the baked asparagus bundles with balsamic glaze just before serving.

Serve the Prosciutto-Wrapped Asparagus with Balsamic Glaze as a delightful appetizer or side dish for any occasion.

Enjoy the combination of salty prosciutto, tender asparagus, and sweet balsamic glaze!

Mediterranean Grilled Veggie Sandwich

Ingredients:

For the Grilled Vegetables:

- 1 zucchini, sliced lengthwise into strips
- 1 yellow squash, sliced lengthwise into strips
- 1 red bell pepper, halved and deseeded
- 1 yellow bell pepper, halved and deseeded
- 1 small eggplant, sliced into rounds
- 1 red onion, sliced into rounds
- 2 tablespoons olive oil
- Salt and pepper to taste
- 1 teaspoon dried oregano
- 1 teaspoon dried thyme

For the Sandwich:

- 4 ciabatta rolls or sandwich buns
- 1/2 cup hummus
- 1/4 cup sun-dried tomatoes, drained and chopped
- 1/4 cup Kalamata olives, pitted and sliced
- Handful of fresh spinach leaves
- 4 slices of provolone cheese (optional)

Instructions:

Preheat your grill or grill pan over medium-high heat.
In a large bowl, toss the sliced zucchini, yellow squash, bell peppers, eggplant, and red onion with olive oil, salt, pepper, dried oregano, and dried thyme until evenly coated.
Grill the vegetables in batches, turning occasionally, until they are tender and lightly charred, about 5-7 minutes per side. Remove from the grill and set aside.
Cut the ciabatta rolls or sandwich buns in half horizontally. If desired, lightly toast the cut sides on the grill or in a toaster.

Spread a generous layer of hummus on the bottom half of each ciabatta roll or sandwich bun.

Layer the grilled vegetables on top of the hummus, followed by the chopped sun-dried tomatoes, sliced Kalamata olives, and fresh spinach leaves.

If using, place a slice of provolone cheese on top of the vegetables.

Place the top half of each ciabatta roll or sandwich bun on top to form sandwiches.

Serve the Mediterranean Grilled Veggie Sandwiches immediately, and enjoy the delicious flavors of the Mediterranean in every bite!

You can also wrap the sandwiches in parchment paper or foil for a picnic or on-the-go meal.

Beef Bulgogi Bibimbap Bowl

Ingredients:

For the Beef Bulgogi:

- 1 pound (450g) beef sirloin or ribeye, thinly sliced
- 1/4 cup soy sauce
- 2 tablespoons brown sugar
- 2 tablespoons sesame oil
- 2 cloves garlic, minced
- 1 teaspoon grated ginger
- 2 green onions, chopped
- 1 tablespoon toasted sesame seeds
- 1 tablespoon rice vinegar
- 1 tablespoon mirin (optional)
- 1 tablespoon vegetable oil (for cooking)

For the Bibimbap Bowl:

- Cooked white rice
- Beef bulgogi (prepared as per the above recipe)
- 4 cups mixed vegetables (such as spinach, carrots, bean sprouts, mushrooms, and zucchini)
- 4 large eggs
- Kimchi (optional, for serving)
- Gochujang (Korean chili paste, optional, for serving)
- Toasted sesame seeds, for garnish
- Sliced green onions, for garnish
- Sesame oil, for drizzling

Instructions:

Marinate the thinly sliced beef: In a bowl, combine soy sauce, brown sugar, sesame oil, minced garlic, grated ginger, chopped green onions, toasted sesame seeds, rice vinegar, and mirin (if using). Add the thinly sliced beef and marinate for at least 30 minutes, or preferably overnight in the refrigerator.

Cook the marinated beef: Heat vegetable oil in a large skillet or wok over medium-high heat. Add the marinated beef and cook for 3-4 minutes until browned and cooked through. Remove from heat and set aside.

Prepare the mixed vegetables: Blanch or sauté the mixed vegetables until tender-crisp. You can blanch spinach, bean sprouts, and carrots, and sauté mushrooms and zucchini.

Cook the eggs: In the same skillet, fry the eggs to your desired doneness (usually sunny side up or over-easy).

Assemble the Bibimbap bowls: Divide the cooked white rice among serving bowls. Arrange the cooked beef bulgogi, mixed vegetables, and fried eggs on top of the rice in separate sections. Add a spoonful of kimchi on the side if desired.

Serve with gochujang: Serve the Bibimbap bowls with gochujang on the side for extra flavor and spice. Drizzle with toasted sesame seeds, sliced green onions, and a drizzle of sesame oil for garnish.

Mix everything together: Before eating, mix all the ingredients in the bowl together with a spoon or chopsticks until well combined. Enjoy your delicious Beef Bulgogi Bibimbap Bowl!

Avocado and Tomato Gazpacho

Ingredients:

- 4 ripe tomatoes, diced
- 1 cucumber, peeled, seeded, and diced
- 1 ripe avocado, peeled, pitted, and diced
- 1/2 red onion, diced
- 1 red bell pepper, diced
- 2 cloves garlic, minced
- 2 tablespoons fresh cilantro, chopped
- 2 tablespoons fresh parsley, chopped
- 3 cups tomato juice or vegetable broth
- 2 tablespoons red wine vinegar
- Juice of 1 lime
- Salt and pepper to taste
- Optional toppings: diced avocado, chopped cilantro, diced cucumber, croutons

Instructions:

In a blender or food processor, combine the diced tomatoes, cucumber, avocado, red onion, red bell pepper, garlic, cilantro, parsley, tomato juice or vegetable broth, red wine vinegar, and lime juice.
Blend until smooth and creamy, scraping down the sides of the blender as needed.
Season the gazpacho with salt and pepper to taste. Adjust the seasoning if needed.
Chill the gazpacho in the refrigerator for at least 1 hour, or until thoroughly chilled.
Before serving, taste the gazpacho again and adjust the seasoning if necessary.
Ladle the chilled gazpacho into serving bowls.
Garnish each bowl with diced avocado, chopped cilantro, diced cucumber, and croutons if desired.
Serve the Avocado and Tomato Gazpacho cold, and enjoy this refreshing and nutritious soup on a hot day!

Pesto Pasta Salad with Cherry Tomatoes

Ingredients:

For the Pesto:

- 2 cups fresh basil leaves, packed
- 1/3 cup pine nuts or walnuts
- 3 cloves garlic, minced
- 1/2 cup grated Parmesan cheese
- 1/2 cup extra-virgin olive oil
- Salt and pepper to taste

For the Pasta Salad:

- 12 oz (340g) pasta of your choice (such as fusilli, penne, or rotini)
- 1 pint cherry tomatoes, halved
- 1/2 cup sliced black olives
- 1/4 cup diced red onion
- 1/4 cup chopped fresh basil leaves
- 1/4 cup grated Parmesan cheese (optional)
- Salt and pepper to taste

Instructions:

Prepare the pesto: In a food processor, combine the basil leaves, pine nuts or walnuts, minced garlic, and grated Parmesan cheese. Pulse until coarsely chopped.
With the food processor running, slowly drizzle in the olive oil until the pesto is smooth and well combined. Season with salt and pepper to taste. Set aside.
Cook the pasta according to the package instructions until al dente. Drain the pasta and rinse it under cold water to stop the cooking process. Transfer the cooked pasta to a large mixing bowl.
Add the halved cherry tomatoes, sliced black olives, diced red onion, chopped fresh basil leaves, and grated Parmesan cheese (if using) to the bowl with the cooked pasta.

Pour the prepared pesto over the pasta and vegetables. Toss everything together until the pasta and vegetables are evenly coated with the pesto.

Season the pasta salad with salt and pepper to taste. Adjust the seasoning if needed.

Cover the bowl and refrigerate the pesto pasta salad for at least 30 minutes to allow the flavors to meld together.

Before serving, give the pasta salad a final toss and taste for seasoning. Adjust as necessary.

Serve the Pesto Pasta Salad with Cherry Tomatoes cold or at room temperature as a delicious side dish or light meal.

Enjoy this flavorful and vibrant pasta salad with the bright flavors of basil pesto and juicy cherry tomatoes!

Crab Stuffed Avocado

Ingredients:

- 2 ripe avocados
- 1 cup lump crab meat, drained and picked over for shells
- 2 tablespoons mayonnaise
- 1 tablespoon chopped fresh parsley
- 1 tablespoon chopped fresh chives (or green onions)
- 1 tablespoon lemon juice
- 1/4 teaspoon Old Bay seasoning (optional)
- Salt and pepper to taste
- Lemon wedges for serving
- Additional chopped parsley or chives for garnish

Instructions:

Cut the avocados in half lengthwise and remove the pits. Scoop out a little bit of the avocado flesh from each half to create a larger cavity for the crab filling, leaving a border around the edges.

In a mixing bowl, combine the lump crab meat, mayonnaise, chopped parsley, chopped chives (or green onions), lemon juice, and Old Bay seasoning (if using). Season with salt and pepper to taste.

Gently fold the crab mixture until well combined.

Spoon the crab mixture evenly into the hollowed-out avocado halves, mounding it slightly on top.

Garnish the stuffed avocados with additional chopped parsley or chives, if desired.

Serve the Crab Stuffed Avocado halves immediately, with lemon wedges on the side for squeezing over the top.

Enjoy this delicious and elegant appetizer or light meal, perfect for any occasion!

Smoked Salmon Bagel with Cream Cheese

Ingredients:

- 2 bagels, sliced and toasted
- 4 oz (about 113g) smoked salmon slices
- 4 tablespoons cream cheese
- 1 tablespoon capers, drained
- 1/4 red onion, thinly sliced
- Fresh dill, for garnish
- Lemon wedges, for serving (optional)

Instructions:

Spread 2 tablespoons of cream cheese evenly onto each toasted bagel half.
Place a layer of smoked salmon slices on top of the cream cheese on each bagel half.
Sprinkle the drained capers over the smoked salmon.
Arrange a few slices of thinly sliced red onion on top of the capers.
Garnish each bagel with fresh dill.
Serve the Smoked Salmon Bagel with Cream Cheese immediately, with lemon wedges on the side for squeezing over the top if desired.
Enjoy this classic and delicious bagel sandwich for breakfast, brunch, or any time of the day!

Vegetable Frittata with Goat Cheese

Ingredients:

- 8 large eggs
- 1/4 cup milk or cream
- Salt and pepper to taste
- 2 tablespoons olive oil
- 1 small onion, diced
- 1 bell pepper, diced
- 1 cup diced vegetables (such as zucchini, mushrooms, spinach, or cherry tomatoes)
- 2 ounces goat cheese, crumbled
- Fresh herbs (such as parsley, chives, or basil), chopped, for garnish

Instructions:

Preheat your oven to 350°F (175°C).
In a large mixing bowl, whisk together the eggs, milk or cream, salt, and pepper until well combined. Set aside.
Heat the olive oil in a large oven-safe skillet over medium heat.
Add the diced onion and bell pepper to the skillet and cook until softened, about 3-4 minutes.
Add the diced vegetables to the skillet and cook until they are tender, about 5-6 minutes. If using spinach, add it last and cook until wilted.
Pour the egg mixture evenly over the cooked vegetables in the skillet.
Crumble the goat cheese over the top of the frittata.
Let the frittata cook undisturbed on the stovetop for 2-3 minutes, or until the edges begin to set.
Transfer the skillet to the preheated oven and bake the frittata for 12-15 minutes, or until the eggs are set in the center and the top is lightly golden brown.
Remove the skillet from the oven and let the frittata cool slightly.
Sprinkle chopped fresh herbs over the top for garnish.
Slice the Vegetable Frittata with Goat Cheese into wedges and serve warm or at room temperature.
Enjoy this flavorful and nutritious dish for breakfast, brunch, or any meal of the day!

Spicy Tuna Poke Bowl

Ingredients:

For the Spicy Tuna:

- 1 lb (450g) sushi-grade tuna, diced
- 2 tablespoons soy sauce
- 1 tablespoon sesame oil
- 1 tablespoon sriracha sauce (adjust to taste)
- 1 teaspoon rice vinegar
- 1 teaspoon honey
- 1 teaspoon grated ginger
- 1 clove garlic, minced
- 2 green onions, thinly sliced
- Sesame seeds, for garnish

For the Bowl:

- 3 cups cooked sushi rice
- 1 avocado, sliced
- 1 cucumber, sliced
- 1/2 cup shredded carrots
- 1/4 cup edamame beans, cooked
- 1/4 cup sliced radishes
- 1/4 cup sliced green onions
- Nori strips, for garnish
- Additional sriracha sauce, for drizzling (optional)

Instructions:

In a mixing bowl, combine diced tuna, soy sauce, sesame oil, sriracha sauce, rice vinegar, honey, grated ginger, minced garlic, and sliced green onions. Toss gently to coat the tuna evenly in the marinade. Adjust the amount of sriracha sauce to your desired level of spiciness. Let it marinate in the refrigerator for at least 15-30 minutes.

Meanwhile, prepare the other ingredients for the bowl. Cook sushi rice according to package instructions. Divide the cooked rice into serving bowls.

Arrange sliced avocado, cucumber, shredded carrots, edamame beans, sliced radishes, and sliced green onions on top of the rice in each bowl.

Once the tuna is marinated, divide it among the bowls, placing it on top of the other ingredients.

Garnish each bowl with nori strips and sesame seeds.

Optionally, drizzle additional sriracha sauce over the top for extra spice.

Serve the Spicy Tuna Poke Bowls immediately and enjoy the delicious flavors and textures!

Roast Beef and Arugula Sandwich with Horseradish Aioli

Ingredients:

For the Horseradish Aioli:

- 1/4 cup mayonnaise
- 1 tablespoon prepared horseradish
- 1 clove garlic, minced
- 1 teaspoon lemon juice
- Salt and pepper to taste

For the Sandwich:

- 4 slices of your favorite bread (such as ciabatta or sourdough), toasted
- 8 oz (225g) thinly sliced roast beef
- 1 cup fresh arugula leaves
- 1/2 red onion, thinly sliced
- 1 tomato, thinly sliced
- 4 slices provolone cheese (optional)

Instructions:

Prepare the Horseradish Aioli: In a small bowl, combine mayonnaise, prepared horseradish, minced garlic, lemon juice, salt, and pepper. Stir until well combined. Adjust seasoning to taste. Set aside.
Assemble the Sandwich: Spread a generous amount of horseradish aioli on one side of each toasted bread slice.
Layer the roast beef slices on two of the bread slices.
Top the roast beef with fresh arugula leaves, thinly sliced red onion, and tomato slices.
If using, add a slice of provolone cheese on top of the vegetables.
Place the remaining bread slices on top to complete the sandwiches.
Cut the sandwiches in half, if desired, and serve immediately.
Enjoy your delicious Roast Beef and Arugula Sandwiches with Horseradish Aioli!

Sweet Potato and Black Bean Quesadilla

Ingredients:

- 1 large sweet potato, peeled and diced
- 1 can (15 oz) black beans, drained and rinsed
- 1 teaspoon ground cumin
- 1/2 teaspoon chili powder
- 1/2 teaspoon paprika
- Salt and pepper to taste
- 4 large flour tortillas
- 1 cup shredded cheese (cheddar, Monterey Jack, or a Mexican blend)
- 1/4 cup chopped fresh cilantro (optional)
- Salsa, guacamole, sour cream, or Greek yogurt for serving (optional)

Instructions:

Steam or boil the diced sweet potato until tender, about 10-15 minutes. Drain and set aside.
In a mixing bowl, mash the black beans with a fork or potato masher until slightly chunky.
Add the cooked sweet potato to the mashed black beans. Stir in the ground cumin, chili powder, paprika, salt, and pepper, mixing until well combined.
Heat a large skillet or griddle over medium heat. Place one tortilla in the skillet and spread a quarter of the sweet potato and black bean mixture evenly over half of the tortilla.
Sprinkle a quarter of the shredded cheese and chopped cilantro (if using) over the sweet potato and black bean mixture.
Fold the other half of the tortilla over the filling to create a half-moon shape. Press down gently with a spatula.
Cook the quesadilla for 2-3 minutes on each side, or until golden brown and crispy, and the cheese is melted.
Repeat the process with the remaining tortillas and filling ingredients.
Once cooked, transfer the quesadillas to a cutting board and let them cool for a minute before slicing into wedges.
Serve the Sweet Potato and Black Bean Quesadillas hot, with salsa, guacamole, sour cream, or Greek yogurt on the side for dipping, if desired.
Enjoy your delicious and satisfying vegetarian quesadillas!

Mediterranean Couscous Salad with Olives and Feta

Ingredients:

For the Salad:

- 1 cup couscous
- 1 1/4 cups vegetable broth or water
- 1 cup cherry tomatoes, halved
- 1/2 English cucumber, diced
- 1/4 cup Kalamata olives, pitted and sliced
- 1/4 cup crumbled feta cheese
- 2 tablespoons chopped fresh parsley
- 2 tablespoons chopped fresh mint (optional)
- Salt and pepper to taste

For the Dressing:

- 3 tablespoons extra virgin olive oil
- 2 tablespoons lemon juice
- 1 teaspoon Dijon mustard
- 1 clove garlic, minced
- 1/2 teaspoon dried oregano
- Salt and pepper to taste

Instructions:

In a medium saucepan, bring the vegetable broth or water to a boil. Stir in the couscous, cover, and remove from heat. Let it sit for 5 minutes, then fluff the couscous with a fork and let it cool to room temperature.
In a large mixing bowl, combine the cooked and cooled couscous with the cherry tomatoes, diced cucumber, Kalamata olives, crumbled feta cheese, chopped parsley, and chopped mint (if using). Toss gently to combine.
In a small bowl, whisk together the extra virgin olive oil, lemon juice, Dijon mustard, minced garlic, dried oregano, salt, and pepper until well combined.
Pour the dressing over the couscous salad and toss until everything is evenly coated.
Taste and adjust seasoning if needed with more salt, pepper, or lemon juice.

Cover the bowl and refrigerate the Mediterranean Couscous Salad for at least 30 minutes to allow the flavors to meld together.
Before serving, give the salad a final toss and garnish with additional chopped parsley or mint if desired.
Serve the Mediterranean Couscous Salad with Olives and Feta chilled or at room temperature as a refreshing and satisfying side dish or light meal.
Enjoy the vibrant flavors of the Mediterranean in every bite!

Thai Coconut Curry Soup with Shrimp

Ingredients:

- 1 tablespoon coconut oil or vegetable oil
- 1 small onion, finely chopped
- 2 cloves garlic, minced
- 1 tablespoon grated fresh ginger
- 2 tablespoons Thai red curry paste
- 4 cups chicken or vegetable broth
- 1 can (14 oz) coconut milk
- 1 tablespoon soy sauce or fish sauce
- 1 tablespoon brown sugar or coconut sugar
- 1 red bell pepper, thinly sliced
- 1 cup sliced mushrooms
- 1 cup baby corn, halved
- 1 cup snow peas, trimmed
- 1 pound (450g) medium shrimp, peeled and deveined
- Juice of 1 lime
- Salt and pepper to taste
- Fresh cilantro leaves, for garnish
- Red chili flakes, for garnish (optional)

Instructions:

In a large pot or Dutch oven, heat the coconut oil over medium heat. Add the chopped onion and cook until softened, about 3-4 minutes.

Add the minced garlic and grated ginger to the pot, and cook for another 1-2 minutes until fragrant.

Stir in the Thai red curry paste and cook for 1 minute, stirring constantly to toast the spices.

Pour in the chicken or vegetable broth and coconut milk, and stir to combine. Bring the soup to a simmer.

Add the soy sauce or fish sauce and brown sugar or coconut sugar to the pot, and stir until the sugar is dissolved.

Add the sliced red bell pepper, mushrooms, baby corn, and snow peas to the soup. Simmer for 5-7 minutes, or until the vegetables are tender-crisp.

Add the peeled and deveined shrimp to the pot, and cook for 3-4 minutes until pink and cooked through.
Stir in the lime juice, and season the soup with salt and pepper to taste.
Ladle the Thai Coconut Curry Soup with Shrimp into bowls, and garnish with fresh cilantro leaves and red chili flakes (if using).
Serve the soup hot, and enjoy the rich and aromatic flavors of Thai cuisine!

Teriyaki Chicken Lettuce Wraps

Ingredients:

For the Teriyaki Chicken:

- 1 lb (450g) boneless, skinless chicken breasts, diced
- 1/4 cup soy sauce
- 2 tablespoons honey or maple syrup
- 2 tablespoons rice vinegar
- 1 tablespoon sesame oil
- 2 cloves garlic, minced
- 1 teaspoon grated ginger
- 1 tablespoon cornstarch
- 2 tablespoons water
- Sesame seeds and sliced green onions for garnish

For the Lettuce Wraps:

- Large lettuce leaves (such as butter lettuce or iceberg lettuce)
- Cooked white rice or quinoa (optional)
- Thinly sliced cucumber
- Shredded carrots
- Sliced bell peppers
- Sliced avocado
- Sriracha or chili garlic sauce (optional, for extra spice)

Instructions:

In a small bowl, whisk together soy sauce, honey or maple syrup, rice vinegar, sesame oil, minced garlic, and grated ginger to make the teriyaki sauce.
In a separate bowl, mix cornstarch and water until smooth to create a slurry.
Heat a large skillet or wok over medium-high heat. Add the diced chicken to the skillet and cook until browned and cooked through, about 5-7 minutes.
Pour the teriyaki sauce over the cooked chicken in the skillet. Stir to coat the chicken evenly.

Add the cornstarch slurry to the skillet and stir well. Cook for another 1-2 minutes, until the sauce thickens and coats the chicken.

Remove the skillet from heat and sprinkle sesame seeds and sliced green onions over the teriyaki chicken for garnish.

To assemble the lettuce wraps, place a spoonful of cooked white rice or quinoa (if using) onto each lettuce leaf.

Top the rice with a generous portion of teriyaki chicken, and add sliced cucumber, shredded carrots, sliced bell peppers, and sliced avocado on top.

Drizzle Sriracha or chili garlic sauce over the filling for extra spice, if desired.

Fold the lettuce leaves around the filling to form wraps, and secure with toothpicks if needed.

Serve the Teriyaki Chicken Lettuce Wraps immediately, and enjoy this flavorful and healthy dish!

Quinoa Salad with Roasted Vegetables and Feta

Ingredients:

For the Roasted Vegetables:

- 2 cups diced vegetables (such as bell peppers, zucchini, eggplant, cherry tomatoes, and red onion)
- 2 tablespoons olive oil
- 1 teaspoon dried herbs (such as thyme, rosemary, or Italian seasoning)
- Salt and pepper to taste

For the Quinoa Salad:

- 1 cup quinoa, rinsed
- 2 cups water or vegetable broth
- 1/4 cup chopped fresh parsley
- 1/4 cup chopped fresh basil
- 1/4 cup chopped fresh mint (optional)
- 1/4 cup crumbled feta cheese
- 1/4 cup sliced Kalamata olives (optional)
- 2 tablespoons lemon juice
- 2 tablespoons extra virgin olive oil
- Salt and pepper to taste

Instructions:

Preheat the oven to 400°F (200°C). Line a baking sheet with parchment paper or aluminum foil for easy cleanup.
In a large mixing bowl, toss the diced vegetables with olive oil, dried herbs, salt, and pepper until evenly coated.
Spread the seasoned vegetables in a single layer on the prepared baking sheet. Roast in the preheated oven for 20-25 minutes, or until tender and slightly caramelized, stirring halfway through the cooking time. Remove from the oven and let cool slightly.
While the vegetables are roasting, rinse the quinoa under cold water using a fine mesh strainer. In a medium saucepan, combine the rinsed quinoa with water or

vegetable broth. Bring to a boil over medium-high heat, then reduce the heat to low, cover, and simmer for 15-20 minutes, or until the quinoa is tender and the liquid is absorbed. Remove from heat and let it sit, covered, for 5 minutes. Fluff the quinoa with a fork and let it cool slightly.

In a large mixing bowl, combine the cooked quinoa, roasted vegetables, chopped parsley, chopped basil, chopped mint (if using), crumbled feta cheese, and sliced Kalamata olives (if using).

In a small bowl, whisk together the lemon juice and extra virgin olive oil to make the dressing. Season with salt and pepper to taste.

Pour the dressing over the quinoa salad and toss until everything is evenly coated.

Taste and adjust seasoning if needed with more salt, pepper, or lemon juice.

Serve the Quinoa Salad with Roasted Vegetables and Feta at room temperature or chilled, and enjoy the delicious combination of flavors and textures!

This salad makes a satisfying and nutritious meal on its own, or it can be served as a side dish or brought to potlucks and gatherings. Enjoy!

Caprese Salad with Balsamic Glaze

Ingredients:

- 2 large ripe tomatoes, sliced
- 8 oz (225g) fresh mozzarella cheese, sliced
- Fresh basil leaves
- Salt and pepper to taste
- Balsamic glaze

Instructions:

Arrange the tomato slices and mozzarella cheese slices alternately on a serving platter, overlapping slightly.

Tuck fresh basil leaves between the tomato and mozzarella slices.

Season the Caprese salad with salt and pepper to taste.

Drizzle balsamic glaze over the assembled salad.

Serve the Caprese Salad with Balsamic Glaze immediately as a refreshing appetizer or side dish.

Enjoy the classic combination of flavors in this simple and elegant salad!

Beef Tenderloin Salad with Blue Cheese Dressing

Ingredients:

For the Beef Tenderloin:

- 1 lb (450g) beef tenderloin
- 2 tablespoons olive oil
- Salt and pepper to taste

For the Salad:

- Mixed salad greens (such as arugula, spinach, and lettuce)
- Cherry tomatoes, halved
- Sliced cucumber
- Sliced red onion
- Crumbled blue cheese
- Toasted walnuts or pecans (optional)

For the Blue Cheese Dressing:

- 1/2 cup mayonnaise
- 1/4 cup sour cream or Greek yogurt
- 1/4 cup crumbled blue cheese
- 1 tablespoon lemon juice
- 1 teaspoon Dijon mustard
- 1 clove garlic, minced
- Salt and pepper to taste

Instructions:

Preheat the oven to 400°F (200°C).
Rub the beef tenderloin with olive oil and season generously with salt and pepper.
Heat a skillet over medium-high heat. Sear the beef tenderloin on all sides until browned, about 2-3 minutes per side.
Transfer the skillet to the preheated oven and roast the beef tenderloin until it reaches your desired level of doneness, about 15-20 minutes for medium-rare

(internal temperature of 135°F or 57°C). Remove from the oven and let it rest for 10 minutes before slicing.

Meanwhile, prepare the salad greens, cherry tomatoes, cucumber, red onion, and toasted walnuts or pecans (if using) on a serving platter.

To make the blue cheese dressing, combine mayonnaise, sour cream or Greek yogurt, crumbled blue cheese, lemon juice, Dijon mustard, minced garlic, salt, and pepper in a bowl. Whisk until smooth and well combined.

Slice the rested beef tenderloin thinly and arrange it on top of the prepared salad.

Drizzle the blue cheese dressing over the beef tenderloin salad.

Serve immediately and enjoy this flavorful and satisfying Beef Tenderloin Salad with Blue Cheese Dressing!

Falafel Wrap with Tahini Sauce

Ingredients:

For the Falafel:

- 1 can (15 oz) chickpeas, drained and rinsed
- 1/2 cup fresh parsley leaves
- 1/2 cup fresh cilantro leaves
- 1/4 cup chopped onion
- 2 cloves garlic, minced
- 1 teaspoon ground cumin
- 1 teaspoon ground coriander
- 1/2 teaspoon baking powder
- Salt and pepper to taste
- 2-3 tablespoons all-purpose flour or chickpea flour (for gluten-free option)
- Olive oil for frying

For the Tahini Sauce:

- 1/4 cup tahini
- 2 tablespoons lemon juice
- 2 tablespoons water
- 1 clove garlic, minced
- Salt to taste

For the Wrap:

- Large flour tortillas or pita bread
- Lettuce leaves
- Sliced tomatoes
- Sliced cucumbers
- Sliced red onions
- Optional extras: pickled turnips, hot sauce, chopped parsley

Instructions:

In a food processor, combine the chickpeas, parsley, cilantro, chopped onion, minced garlic, ground cumin, ground coriander, baking powder, salt, and pepper. Pulse until the mixture is finely chopped and holds together when pressed.

Transfer the falafel mixture to a bowl and stir in 2-3 tablespoons of flour until the mixture is firm enough to form into balls. If the mixture is too wet, add more flour as needed.

Heat olive oil in a skillet over medium heat. Form the falafel mixture into small balls or patties and gently flatten them with your hands. Fry the falafel in batches until golden brown and crispy on both sides, about 3-4 minutes per side. Transfer to a paper towel-lined plate to drain excess oil.

To make the tahini sauce, whisk together tahini, lemon juice, water, minced garlic, and salt in a small bowl until smooth and creamy. Add more water if needed to reach your desired consistency.

Warm the flour tortillas or pita bread in a skillet or microwave.

To assemble the falafel wraps, spread a generous amount of tahini sauce on each tortilla or pita bread. Top with lettuce leaves, sliced tomatoes, sliced cucumbers, sliced red onions, falafel, and any optional extras such as pickled turnips, hot sauce, or chopped parsley.

Roll up the wraps tightly, tucking in the sides as you go.

Serve the Falafel Wraps with Tahini Sauce immediately, and enjoy this delicious and satisfying Mediterranean-inspired meal!

Chicken Satay Skewers with Peanut Sauce

Ingredients:

For the Chicken Satay:

- 1 lb (450g) boneless, skinless chicken breasts or thighs, cut into thin strips
- 2 tablespoons soy sauce
- 2 tablespoons fish sauce
- 2 tablespoons brown sugar or honey
- 1 tablespoon lime juice
- 1 teaspoon ground turmeric
- 1 teaspoon ground cumin
- 1 teaspoon ground coriander
- 2 cloves garlic, minced
- 1 tablespoon vegetable oil
- Wooden skewers, soaked in water for 30 minutes

For the Peanut Sauce:

- 1/2 cup creamy peanut butter
- 1/4 cup coconut milk
- 2 tablespoons soy sauce
- 1 tablespoon lime juice
- 1 tablespoon brown sugar or honey
- 1 teaspoon grated ginger
- 1 clove garlic, minced
- 1 teaspoon sriracha sauce or chili garlic sauce (optional)
- Water, as needed to thin out the sauce

Instructions:

In a mixing bowl, combine soy sauce, fish sauce, brown sugar or honey, lime juice, ground turmeric, ground cumin, ground coriander, minced garlic, and vegetable oil. Stir until well combined.

Add the chicken strips to the marinade and toss until evenly coated. Cover and refrigerate for at least 30 minutes, or up to 2 hours, to allow the flavors to meld together.

While the chicken is marinating, prepare the peanut sauce. In a small saucepan over low heat, combine peanut butter, coconut milk, soy sauce, lime juice, brown sugar or honey, grated ginger, minced garlic, and sriracha sauce or chili garlic sauce (if using). Stir until the peanut butter is melted and the sauce is smooth. If the sauce is too thick, add water a little at a time until it reaches your desired consistency. Keep warm over low heat until ready to serve.

Preheat a grill or grill pan over medium-high heat. Thread the marinated chicken strips onto the soaked wooden skewers.

Grill the chicken skewers for 3-4 minutes on each side, or until cooked through and lightly charred. Make sure to turn them occasionally to ensure even cooking.

Transfer the grilled chicken satay skewers to a serving platter and serve immediately with the warm peanut sauce on the side for dipping.

Enjoy the delicious flavors of these Chicken Satay Skewers with Peanut Sauce as an appetizer, main dish, or party snack!

Veggie Sushi Bowl with Ginger Soy Dressing

Ingredients:

For the Veggie Sushi Bowl:

- 2 cups sushi rice, cooked according to package instructions
- 1 large carrot, julienned
- 1 cucumber, julienned
- 1 avocado, sliced
- 1/2 red bell pepper, thinly sliced
- 1/2 yellow bell pepper, thinly sliced
- 1/2 cup shelled edamame
- 1 nori sheet, thinly sliced or crumbled
- Sesame seeds, for garnish
- Pickled ginger, for serving (optional)
- Wasabi, for serving (optional)

For the Ginger Soy Dressing:

- 1/4 cup soy sauce
- 2 tablespoons rice vinegar
- 1 tablespoon sesame oil
- 1 tablespoon grated fresh ginger
- 1 tablespoon honey or maple syrup
- 1 garlic clove, minced
- 1 tablespoon water

Instructions:

In a small bowl, whisk together all the ingredients for the Ginger Soy Dressing until well combined. Set aside.
Divide the cooked sushi rice among serving bowls.
Arrange the julienned carrot, cucumber, sliced avocado, sliced red bell pepper, sliced yellow bell pepper, and shelled edamame on top of the sushi rice in each bowl.
Drizzle the Ginger Soy Dressing over the veggie sushi bowls.
Garnish each bowl with thinly sliced or crumbled nori and sesame seeds.

Serve the Veggie Sushi Bowls with additional pickled ginger and wasabi on the side if desired.

Enjoy these delicious and nutritious Veggie Sushi Bowls with Ginger Soy Dressing as a healthy and satisfying meal!